Table Of Contents

    What is Lead Generation? 2
    The Importance of Lead Generation for Website Owners 2
    Common Lead Generation Mistakes to Avoid 2
Chapter 2: Leveraging Social Media for Lead Generation 2
    The Role of Social Media in Lead Generation 2
    Choosing the Right Social Media Platforms 2
    Creating Engaging Content for Lead Generation 2
Chapter 3: Building a Strong Social Media Strategy 2
    Setting Clear Goals for Lead Generation 2
    Identifying Your Target Audience 2
    Developing a Content Calendar for Consistent Lead Generation 2
Chapter 4: Implementing Lead Generation Tactics on Social Media 2
    Using Paid Advertising for Lead Generation 2
    Leveraging Influencer Marketing for Lead Generation 2
    Utilizing Social Media Contests and Giveaways 2
Chapter 5: Measuring and Analyzing Lead Generation Results 2
    Tracking Key Metrics for Lead Generation Success 2
    Analyzing Data to Improve Lead Generation Efforts 2
    Adjusting Your Social Media Strategy for Better Lead Generation Results.2
Chapter 6: Case Studies and Success Stories 2
    Case Study: How Company A Generated Leads with Social Media 2
    Success Story: The Impact of Social Media on Lead Generation for Company B 2
Chapter 7: Future Trends in Social Media Lead Generation 2
    The Rise of Chatbots in Lead Generation 2
    Personalization and Customization in Social Media Lead Generation .. 2
    The Role of AI in Enhancing Lead Generation Strategies 2
Chapter 8: Conclusion 2
    Recap of Key Strategies for Successful Lead Generation on Social Media..2
    Final Thoughts on Cracking the Code to Lead Generation with Social Media 2
Chapter 1: Understanding the Basics of Lead Generation 1

Chapter 1: Understanding the Basics of Lead Generation

What is Lead Generation?

Lead generation is a critical aspect of any successful marketing strategy. It involves identifying and attracting potential customers to your business with the goal of converting them into leads. In simple terms, lead generation is the process of creating interest in your products or services among your target audience. This can be done through various marketing tactics, such as social media campaigns, email marketing, and content marketing.

For website owners, marketing professionals, and online marketers, lead generation is essential for driving traffic to their websites and ultimately increasing sales. By generating leads through social media platforms, businesses can reach a wider audience and engage with potential customers on a more personal level. Social media allows marketers to create targeted campaigns that appeal to specific demographics, making it easier to attract qualified leads.

One of the key benefits of using social media for lead generation is the ability to track and measure the success of your campaigns. By analyzing metrics such as click-through rates, conversion rates, and engagement levels, marketers can gain valuable insights into which strategies are most effective in generating leads. This data can then be used to fine-tune future campaigns and maximize their impact.

In today's digital age, social media has become a powerful tool for lead generation. With millions of users active on platforms like Facebook, Instagram, and LinkedIn, businesses have a unique opportunity to connect with potential customers in a more personal and direct way. By creating compelling content, engaging with followers, and running targeted ads, marketers can effectively generate leads and drive sales for their businesses.

In conclusion, lead generation is a crucial aspect of any successful marketing strategy, especially for website owners, marketing professionals, and online marketers looking to generate leads with social media. By leveraging the power of social media platforms, businesses can reach a wider audience, engage with potential customers, and ultimately drive sales. By understanding the fundamentals of lead generation and implementing effective strategies, marketers can unlock the potential of social media as a powerful tool for generating leads.

The Importance of Lead Generation for Website Owners

Lead generation is a critical component for website owners looking to grow their online presence and reach their target audience. In today's digital age, where competition is fierce and attention spans are short, it is more important than ever to capture the interest of potential customers and convert them into leads. By implementing effective lead generation strategies, website owners can increase traffic to their site, build brand awareness, and ultimately drive sales.

One of the key reasons lead generation is so important for website owners is that it helps them identify and target potential customers who are interested in their products or services. By capturing the contact information of these leads, website owners can nurture them through the sales funnel and ultimately convert them into paying customers. This targeted approach not only increases the likelihood of making a sale, but also helps to build long-term relationships with customers, leading to repeat business and referrals.

Lead generation also allows website owners to track and measure the effectiveness of their marketing efforts. By monitoring key metrics such as conversion rates, click-through rates, and lead quality, website owners can gain valuable insights into which strategies are working and which need to be adjusted. This data-driven approach enables website owners to optimize their marketing campaigns for maximum impact, ultimately leading to higher ROI and increased revenue.

In addition to driving sales and measuring success, lead generation also helps website owners build credibility and authority in their niche. By consistently providing valuable content and engaging with their audience through social media, website owners can position themselves as industry experts and thought leaders. This not only helps to attract more leads, but also establishes trust and loyalty with customers, making it more likely that they will choose to do business with the website owner over competitors.

Overall, lead generation is an essential aspect of any website owner's marketing strategy. By focusing on generating and nurturing leads through social media and other channels, website owners can increase brand awareness, drive sales, and build long-term relationships with customers. By understanding the importance of lead generation and implementing effective strategies, website owners can unlock the full potential of their online presence and achieve sustainable growth in their business.

Common Lead Generation Mistakes to Avoid

In the world of online marketing, lead generation is crucial for the success of any business. However, many website owners and marketers often make common mistakes that can hinder their efforts to generate leads effectively. In this subchapter, we will discuss some of the most common lead generation mistakes to avoid in order to maximize your success in generating leads through social media.

One of the most common lead generation mistakes to avoid is not having a clear and concise call-to-action on your website or social media platforms. A call-to-action is essential for guiding potential customers on the next steps to take, whether it's signing up for a newsletter, downloading a free ebook, or making a purchase. Without a clear call-to-action, visitors may not know what action to take, resulting in missed opportunities for lead generation.

Another common mistake is not optimizing your website or social media profiles for lead generation. This includes having a cluttered and confusing layout, slow loading times, or outdated information. By optimizing your online presence for lead generation, you can ensure that visitors have a seamless experience and are more likely to convert into leads.

Furthermore, many marketers make the mistake of not using social media effectively for lead generation. Social media platforms offer a wealth of opportunities for reaching potential customers and generating leads, but it's important to use them strategically. Posting consistently, engaging with followers, and using targeted advertising can all help increase your lead generation efforts through social media.

Additionally, failing to track and analyze your lead generation efforts is another common mistake that can hinder your success. Without tracking and analyzing key metrics such as conversion rates, click-through rates, and engagement levels, you won't know what is working and what isn't. By regularly monitoring and analyzing your lead generation efforts, you can make informed decisions to optimize your strategies and improve your results.

In conclusion, by avoiding these common lead generation mistakes and implementing effective strategies, website owners and marketers can maximize their success in generating leads through social media. By having clear calls-to-action, optimizing your online presence, using social media strategically, and tracking and analyzing your efforts, you can improve your lead generation efforts and ultimately drive more conversions for your business.

Chapter 2: Leveraging Social Media for Lead Generation

The Role of Social Media in Lead Generation

Social media has become an integral part of the lead generation process for businesses of all sizes. In today's digital age, social media platforms such as Facebook, Twitter, Instagram, and LinkedIn play a crucial role in connecting businesses with their target audience and driving traffic to their websites. This subchapter will explore the role of social media in lead generation and provide valuable insights and strategies for website owners, marketing professionals, and online marketers looking to leverage social media to generate leads.

One of the key advantages of using social media for lead generation is its ability to reach a wide audience quickly and cost-effectively. With billions of users actively engaging on social media platforms every day, businesses can tap into this vast pool of potential leads by creating targeted and engaging content that resonates with their target audience. By leveraging the power of social media algorithms and analytics, businesses can track and analyze the performance of their campaigns in real-time, allowing them to optimize their strategies for maximum impact.

Moreover, social media platforms offer a range of tools and features that can help businesses capture leads and drive conversions. For example, Facebook and Instagram offer lead generation ads that allow businesses to collect valuable customer information directly from their social media profiles. By creating compelling ad campaigns and targeting specific audience segments, businesses can attract high-quality leads and nurture them through the sales funnel.

In addition to paid advertising, businesses can also leverage organic social media strategies to generate leads. By creating and sharing valuable content such as blog posts, videos, and infographics, businesses can attract and engage their target audience, building trust and credibility over time. By actively engaging with followers, responding to comments and messages, and participating in industry discussions, businesses can establish themselves as thought leaders in their niche and drive organic traffic to their websites.

In conclusion, social media plays a crucial role in lead generation for website owners, marketing professionals, and online marketers. By leveraging the power of social media platforms, businesses can reach a wide audience, capture leads, and drive conversions effectively and efficiently. By developing a comprehensive social media strategy that combines paid advertising with organic content marketing, businesses can generate high-quality leads and build lasting relationships with their target audience.

Choosing the Right Social Media Platforms

Choosing the right social media platforms is crucial for website owners, marketing professionals, and online marketers looking to generate leads through social media. With so many platforms available, it can be overwhelming to decide where to focus your efforts. However, by understanding your target audience and the unique features of each platform, you can make informed decisions that will maximize your lead generation efforts.

One of the first steps in choosing the right social media platforms is to understand your target audience. Different demographics tend to gravitate towards different platforms, so it's important to know where your ideal customers are spending their time online. For example, if you are targeting a younger audience, platforms like Instagram and TikTok may be more effective than LinkedIn or Facebook. By knowing your audience, you can tailor your content and engagement strategies to reach them where they are most active.

Another important factor to consider when choosing social media platforms is the unique features and strengths of each platform. For example, Instagram is known for its visual content and influencer partnerships, making it a great platform for showcasing products and building brand awareness. On the other hand, LinkedIn is more business-focused and can be a valuable tool for networking and establishing thought leadership in your industry. By understanding the strengths of each platform, you can choose the ones that align most closely with your goals and target audience.

It's also important to consider your own resources and bandwidth when choosing social media platforms. Each platform requires a certain level of time and effort to maintain, so it's important to choose ones that you can effectively manage. If you have limited resources, it may be better to focus on a few key platforms where you can consistently post high-quality content and engage with your audience, rather than spreading yourself too thin across multiple platforms.

In conclusion, choosing the right social media platforms is a critical step in generating leads through social media. By understanding your target audience, the unique features of each platform, and your own resources, you can make informed decisions that will maximize your lead generation efforts. Remember to regularly evaluate your strategies and adjust as needed to ensure that you are reaching your goals and connecting with your audience effectively.

Creating Engaging Content for Lead Generation

Creating engaging content is crucial for lead generation in today's digital age. With the rise of social media platforms, website owners, marketers, and online marketing professionals must adapt their strategies to capture the attention of their target audience. In this subchapter, we will explore the best practices for creating content that resonates with your audience and drives lead generation.

One of the key elements of creating engaging content is understanding your target audience. By conducting thorough research and analyzing your target demographic, you can tailor your content to meet their needs and interests. This will not only help you attract more leads but also build a loyal following of customers who are more likely to convert.

In addition to knowing your audience, it's important to consider the type of content that will resonate with them. Whether it's informative blog posts, eye-catching infographics, or entertaining videos, the key is to create content that is valuable and relevant to your target audience. By providing content that solves their problems or entertains them, you are more likely to capture their attention and generate leads.

Furthermore, it's essential to optimize your content for social media platforms. With the majority of internet users spending hours on various social media channels, it's important to create content that is shareable and engaging. By incorporating visual elements, catchy headlines, and calls to action, you can encourage your audience to interact with your content and share it with their network, ultimately driving more leads to your website.

Another effective strategy for creating engaging content for lead generation is to leverage user-generated content. Encouraging your audience to create and share content related to your brand not only increases engagement but also builds trust and credibility. By showcasing user-generated content on your website and social media channels, you can create a sense of community and authenticity that resonates with your target audience.

Overall, creating engaging content for lead generation requires a deep understanding of your target audience, a variety of content types, optimization for social media platforms, and the integration of user-generated content. By implementing these strategies, website owners, marketers, and online marketing professionals can effectively attract and convert leads through social media channels.

Chapter 3: Building a Strong Social Media Strategy

Setting Clear Goals for Lead Generation

Setting clear goals for lead generation is crucial for success in any marketing strategy, especially when utilizing social media platforms. As website owners and online marketers, it is important to define what success looks like for your lead generation efforts. This includes setting specific, measurable goals that align with your overall business objectives. By clearly defining your goals, you can create a roadmap for your lead generation efforts and track your progress along the way.

One of the key benefits of setting clear goals for lead generation is increased focus and accountability. When you have specific goals in place, you and your team are more likely to stay on track and prioritize activities that will help you achieve those goals. This can help ensure that your lead generation efforts are consistent and effective, leading to better results in the long run. Additionally, clear goals can help you identify areas for improvement and make adjustments to your strategy as needed.

In order to set clear goals for lead generation, it is important to consider both short-term and long-term objectives. Short-term goals may include increasing website traffic, growing your social media following, or capturing email leads. Long-term goals, on the other hand, may involve converting leads into customers, increasing sales revenue, or expanding your market reach. By setting goals that span both timeframes, you can create a holistic lead generation strategy that addresses both immediate and future needs.

When setting goals for lead generation, it is also important to make them SMART: specific, measurable, achievable, relevant, and time-bound. This means that your goals should be clearly defined, quantifiable, realistic, aligned with your business objectives, and have a deadline for completion. By following the SMART criteria, you can ensure that your goals are attainable and provide a clear direction for your lead generation efforts.

In conclusion, setting clear goals for lead generation is essential for website owners and online marketers looking to generate leads using social media. By defining specific, measurable goals that align with your business objectives, you can increase focus, accountability, and effectiveness in your lead generation efforts. Remember to consider both short-term and long-term goals, and make sure they are SMART to set yourself up for success. With clear goals in place, you can create a roadmap for your lead generation strategy and track your progress towards achieving your desired outcomes.

Identifying Your Target Audience

Identifying Your Target Audience is crucial for any successful lead generation strategy. As website owners, marketers, and online marketing professionals, understanding who your audience is and what they are looking for is the key to creating content and campaigns that resonate with them. By identifying your target audience, you can tailor your messaging and offerings to meet their specific needs and preferences, increasing the likelihood of capturing their interest and converting them into leads.

One of the first steps in identifying your target audience is to conduct thorough market research. This involves gathering data on your target demographic, including their age, gender, location, interests, and online behavior. By analyzing this information, you can gain valuable insights into who your audience is and what motivates them to engage with your brand. This data can also help you segment your audience into different groups based on their needs and preferences, allowing you to create targeted campaigns that speak directly to each segment.

In addition to market research, it is important to engage with your audience on social media platforms to gain a better understanding of their interests and preferences. By monitoring conversations, comments, and feedback from your audience, you can identify common themes and trends that can help you tailor your content and messaging to better resonate with them. Social media also provides a valuable platform for testing different messaging and creative approaches to see what resonates best with your target audience.

Another important aspect of identifying your target audience is understanding their pain points and challenges. By identifying the problems your audience is facing, you can position your products or services as solutions that can help alleviate their pain points. This can help you create compelling messaging that speaks directly to your audience's needs and motivates them to take action. By addressing your audience's pain points, you can build trust and credibility with them, increasing the likelihood of converting them into leads.

Ultimately, identifying your target audience is an ongoing process that requires constant monitoring and adjustment. By staying attuned to your audience's needs and preferences, you can continuously optimize your lead generation strategies to ensure they are effective in capturing and converting leads. By taking the time to understand your target audience and craft targeted messaging that resonates with them, you can set yourself up for success in generating leads through social media.

Developing a Content Calendar for Consistent Lead Generation

Developing a content calendar is crucial for consistent lead generation through social media. By planning out your content in advance, you can ensure that you are consistently providing valuable and engaging content to your audience. This will help to keep your followers engaged and interested in what you have to offer, ultimately leading to more leads for your business.

When creating a content calendar, it is important to consider the needs and interests of your target audience. Think about what types of content they would find valuable and engaging, and tailor your content calendar to meet those needs. This will help to ensure that your content is relevant and resonates with your audience, making them more likely to engage with your brand and ultimately become leads for your business.

It is also important to consider the different types of content that you will be sharing on social media. This could include blog posts, videos, infographics, and more. By diversifying your content, you can appeal to a wider range of people and keep your audience interested in what you have to offer. This will help to attract more leads to your business and keep them engaged with your brand over time.

Another important aspect of developing a content calendar for lead generation is consistency. By posting regularly and consistently on social media, you can keep your audience engaged and interested in what you have to offer. This will help to build trust with your audience and ultimately lead to more leads for your business. Make sure to schedule your content in advance and stick to your posting schedule to maximize the effectiveness of your lead generation efforts.

In conclusion, developing a content calendar for lead generation is essential for website owners, marketers, and online marketing professionals looking to generate leads through social media. By planning out your content in advance, considering the needs of your target audience, diversifying your content, and posting consistently, you can attract more leads to your business and keep them engaged with your brand over time. By following these strategies, you can crack the code to lead generation and take your business to the next level.

Chapter 4: Implementing Lead Generation Tactics on Social Media

Using Paid Advertising for Lead Generation

Using paid advertising for lead generation can be an effective strategy for website owners, marketers, and online marketing professionals looking to generate leads through social media. Paid advertising allows you to reach a highly targeted audience and drive traffic to your website or landing page. By investing in paid advertising, you can increase brand awareness, attract new customers, and ultimately grow your business.

One of the key benefits of using paid advertising for lead generation is the ability to target specific demographics, interests, and behaviors. This level of targeting ensures that your ads are seen by the right people who are most likely to be interested in your products or services. By reaching a highly targeted audience, you can increase the likelihood of converting leads into customers and ultimately driving sales.

Another advantage of using paid advertising for lead generation is the ability to track and measure the success of your campaigns. With tools like Google Analytics and Facebook Ads Manager, you can monitor the performance of your ads in real-time and make adjustments as needed to optimize your results. By analyzing key metrics such as click-through rates, conversion rates, and return on investment, you can fine-tune your advertising strategy to maximize your lead generation efforts.

When using paid advertising for lead generation, it's important to create compelling ad copy and visuals that resonate with your target audience. Your ads should clearly communicate the value proposition of your products or services and include a call-to-action that encourages users to take the next step, such as signing up for a free trial or downloading a whitepaper. By creating engaging and relevant ad content, you can capture the attention of potential leads and compel them to learn more about your brand.

In conclusion, using paid advertising for lead generation can be a powerful tool for website owners, marketers, and online marketing professionals looking to generate leads through social media. By targeting specific demographics, tracking and measuring campaign performance, and creating compelling ad content, you can increase brand awareness, attract new customers, and drive sales. With the right strategy and execution, paid advertising can help you unlock the full potential of social media for lead generation and grow your business.

Leveraging Influencer Marketing for Lead Generation

In today's digital age, leveraging influencer marketing has become an essential strategy for website owners and marketers looking to generate leads through social media. Influencer marketing involves partnering with individuals who have a large following on social media platforms to promote your products or services. These influencers have built credibility and trust with their audience, making them powerful advocates for your brand.

One of the key benefits of influencer marketing for lead generation is the ability to reach a highly targeted audience. By partnering with influencers who cater to your niche market, you can ensure that your message reaches the right people who are more likely to be interested in your offerings. This targeted approach can result in higher conversion rates and a better return on investment for your marketing efforts.

Another advantage of influencer marketing is the potential for building brand awareness and credibility. When an influencer promotes your products or services to their audience, it lends a level of authenticity and authority to your brand. This can help to establish trust with potential leads and increase the likelihood of them engaging with your brand.

To effectively leverage influencer marketing for lead generation, it's important to choose the right influencers to partner with. Look for influencers who align with your brand values and have a genuine connection with their audience. Additionally, ensure that the content they create is in line with your marketing objectives and resonates with your target audience.

Overall, influencer marketing can be a powerful tool for website owners and marketers looking to generate leads through social media. By partnering with influencers who have a strong following and credibility, you can reach a targeted audience, build brand awareness, and drive conversions. With the right strategy and approach, influencer marketing can help you crack the code to lead generation in today's competitive digital landscape.

Utilizing Social Media Contests and Giveaways

In today's digital age, social media has become a powerful tool for marketers looking to generate leads and engage with their target audience. One effective strategy that website owners and marketers can utilize is hosting social media contests and giveaways. These interactive campaigns not only help increase brand awareness but also encourage user participation and engagement.

One of the key benefits of running social media contests and giveaways is the ability to reach a wider audience. By requiring participants to like, share, or comment on a post in order to enter the contest, marketers can increase the visibility of their brand and attract new followers. This increased engagement can lead to more traffic to your website and ultimately generate more leads for your business.

Additionally, social media contests and giveaways can help build brand loyalty and trust among your audience. By offering valuable prizes or exclusive discounts, you are showing your customers that you value their support and are willing to reward them for their loyalty. This positive interaction can lead to repeat purchases and referrals, further expanding your customer base and increasing your lead generation efforts.

To ensure the success of your social media contests and giveaways, it is important to set clear goals and objectives. Whether you are looking to increase your number of followers, drive traffic to your website, or collect user-generated content, having a specific goal in mind will help you tailor your campaign to meet those objectives. Additionally, be sure to choose prizes that are relevant to your target audience and align with your brand values to attract the right participants.

In conclusion, social media contests and giveaways are a valuable tool for website owners and marketers looking to generate leads and engage with their audience. By creating interactive campaigns that encourage user participation and offer valuable prizes, you can increase brand awareness, build loyalty, and drive traffic to your website. With careful planning and execution, social media contests and giveaways can be a highly effective strategy for lead generation in today's competitive digital landscape.

Chapter 5: Measuring and Analyzing Lead Generation Results

Tracking Key Metrics for Lead Generation Success

In the world of digital marketing, tracking key metrics is essential for lead generation success. By monitoring and analyzing data, website owners, marketing, and online marketing professionals can gain valuable insights into the effectiveness of their social media strategies. This information allows them to make informed decisions on how to optimize their lead generation campaigns for maximum results.

One of the most important metrics to track for lead generation success is conversion rate. This metric measures the percentage of website visitors who take a desired action, such as signing up for a newsletter or making a purchase. By monitoring conversion rates, marketers can determine which social media channels are driving the most qualified leads and adjust their strategies accordingly.

Another key metric to track is click-through rate (CTR). This metric measures the percentage of people who click on a link or ad after seeing it on social media. A high CTR indicates that the content is engaging and relevant to the target audience, while a low CTR may indicate that changes need to be made to the messaging or targeting.

Engagement metrics, such as likes, comments, and shares, are also important indicators of lead generation success. These metrics provide insight into how well the content resonates with the audience and can help marketers identify which types of posts are most likely to generate leads. By tracking engagement metrics, website owners and marketing professionals can refine their social media strategies to attract and convert more leads.

Finally, tracking lead quality is crucial for determining the overall success of a lead generation campaign. By analyzing the source of leads, their demographics, and their behavior on the website, marketers can identify which leads are most likely to convert into customers. This information can help website owners and marketing professionals focus their efforts on attracting high-quality leads that are more likely to result in sales.

In conclusion, tracking key metrics for lead generation success is essential for website owners, marketing, and online marketing professionals in the niche of generating leads with social media. By monitoring conversion rates, click-through rates, engagement metrics, and lead quality, marketers can optimize their social media strategies to attract and convert more qualified leads. This data-driven approach allows them to make informed decisions that lead to improved lead generation results and ultimately, increased revenue.

Analyzing Data to Improve Lead Generation Efforts

In the digital age, lead generation has become a crucial aspect of any successful marketing strategy. Website owners, marketers, and online marketing professionals are constantly seeking new ways to improve their lead generation efforts. One effective method for achieving this is by analyzing data gathered from social media platforms. By examining key metrics and trends, marketers can gain valuable insights into what is working and what needs improvement in their lead generation campaigns.

One of the first steps in analyzing data for lead generation is to identify the key performance indicators (KPIs) that are most relevant to your goals. These could include metrics such as click-through rates, conversion rates, and engagement levels. By tracking these KPIs over time, marketers can determine which strategies are most effective in generating leads and which may need to be adjusted.

Another important aspect of data analysis for lead generation is segmentation. By dividing your audience into different groups based on demographics, interests, or behaviors, marketers can tailor their messaging and content to better resonate with each segment. This targeted approach can lead to higher conversion rates and ultimately more qualified leads.

In addition to KPIs and segmentation, marketers can also use data analysis to optimize their social media content. By tracking the performance of different types of posts, such as videos, images, or text-based updates, marketers can determine which formats are most engaging to their audience. This information can then be used to create more compelling content that drives leads and conversions.

Overall, analyzing data to improve lead generation efforts is a crucial step in any social media marketing strategy. By tracking KPIs, segmenting your audience, and optimizing your content, marketers can gain valuable insights that lead to more effective lead generation campaigns. By harnessing the power of data, website owners, marketers, and online marketing professionals can take their lead generation efforts to the next level and achieve greater success in generating leads with social media.

Adjusting Your Social Media Strategy for Better Lead Generation Results

In today's digital age, social media has become an essential tool for marketers looking to generate leads and drive sales. However, simply having a presence on social media is not enough. To truly maximize your lead generation efforts, it is important to constantly adjust and refine your social media strategy. In this subchapter, we will explore key strategies for optimizing your social media approach to achieve better lead generation results.

The first step in adjusting your social media strategy for better lead generation results is to clearly define your target audience. Understanding who your ideal customers are will allow you to tailor your content and messaging to resonate with them. Conducting market research and analyzing your existing customer data can help you create buyer personas that will guide your social media efforts.

Once you have identified your target audience, it is important to choose the right social media platforms to reach them. Different platforms cater to different demographics, so it is essential to focus your efforts on the platforms where your target audience is most active. By concentrating your resources on the platforms that are most likely to yield results, you can maximize your lead generation potential.

In addition to choosing the right platforms, it is crucial to create engaging and relevant content that will capture the attention of your target audience. Whether it's informative blog posts, eye-catching images, or interactive videos, your content should be designed to educate, entertain, and inspire your followers. By consistently delivering high-quality content that adds value to your audience, you can build trust and credibility that will ultimately drive leads.

Another key element of adjusting your social media strategy for better lead generation results is to actively engage with your followers. Responding to comments, messages, and mentions in a timely manner shows that you value your audience and are committed to building relationships with them. By fostering a sense of community and interaction on your social media channels, you can increase brand loyalty and encourage followers to take action, such as signing up for a newsletter or making a purchase.

In conclusion, optimizing your social media strategy for lead generation requires a combination of strategic planning, audience targeting, content creation, and engagement. By continuously refining and adjusting your approach based on data and analytics, you can improve your chances of attracting and converting leads through social media. By implementing the strategies outlined in this subchapter, website owners, marketers, and online marketing professionals in the niche of generating leads with social media can achieve better results and drive business growth.

Chapter 6: Case Studies and Success Stories

Case Study: How Company A Generated Leads with Social Media

In this case study, we will delve into how Company A successfully generated leads using social media as part of their marketing strategy. Company A, a leading e-commerce retailer in the fashion industry, was facing a challenge in reaching their target audience and converting them into customers. They turned to social media to increase brand awareness and drive traffic to their website.

Company A started by identifying their target audience and understanding their preferences and behaviors on social media platforms. By conducting thorough market research, they were able to create targeted content that resonated with their audience. They utilized platforms such as Instagram, Facebook, and Pinterest to showcase their products and engage with potential customers.

One of the key strategies that Company A implemented was creating visually appealing content that showcased their products in a lifestyle setting. By using high-quality images and videos, they were able to capture the attention of their audience and drive them to their website. They also utilized influencer partnerships to reach a wider audience and build credibility within their niche.

Through consistent posting and engagement with their followers, Company A was able to build a loyal customer base and increase brand loyalty. They also utilized social media advertising to target specific demographics and drive traffic to their website. By analyzing the performance of their social media campaigns, they were able to optimize their strategies and generate more leads over time.

Overall, Company A's success in generating leads with social media can be attributed to their understanding of their target audience, consistent content creation, and strategic use of social media platforms. By following their example and implementing similar strategies, website owners, marketers, and online marketing professionals can effectively generate leads and drive sales through social media.

Success Story: The Impact of Social Media on Lead Generation for Company B

In today's digital age, social media has become an integral tool for companies looking to generate leads and increase their customer base. Company B is a prime example of how leveraging social media platforms can have a significant impact on lead generation. By implementing strategic social media strategies, Company B was able to not only increase their online presence but also drive traffic to their website and convert leads into loyal customers.

One of the key tactics that Company B used to boost their lead generation efforts was creating engaging and relevant content that resonated with their target audience. By consistently posting informative and visually appealing content on platforms such as Facebook, Twitter, and Instagram, Company B was able to attract the attention of potential customers and establish themselves as industry experts. This helped increase brand awareness and credibility, ultimately leading to a higher conversion rate.

Additionally, Company B made sure to interact with their followers on social media by responding to comments, messages, and inquiries in a timely manner. This level of engagement helped build trust with their audience and fostered strong relationships with customers. By actively listening to feedback and addressing concerns, Company B was able to tailor their marketing strategies to better meet the needs of their target demographic, resulting in a higher lead generation rate.

Another key factor in Company B's success story was their use of targeted advertising on social media platforms. By utilizing tools such as Facebook Ads and Instagram Ads, Company B was able to reach a specific audience based on demographics, interests, and behavior. This helped them connect with potential leads who were more likely to be interested in their products or services, ultimately leading to a higher conversion rate and increased sales.

Overall, the impact of social media on lead generation for Company B was undeniable. By implementing a comprehensive social media strategy that focused on creating valuable content, engaging with followers, and utilizing targeted advertising, Company B was able to significantly increase their online visibility, drive traffic to their website, and convert leads into loyal customers. This success story serves as a testament to the power of social media in today's digital marketing landscape and demonstrates the immense potential it holds for companies looking to grow their business and reach new heights of success.

Chapter 7: Future Trends in Social Media Lead Generation

The Rise of Chatbots in Lead Generation

In recent years, chatbots have become an increasingly popular tool for website owners and marketers looking to generate leads through social media. These automated messaging systems are revolutionizing the way businesses interact with their customers online, providing a more personalized and efficient experience. In this subchapter, we will explore the rise of chatbots in lead generation and how they can benefit those in the online marketing industry.

One of the main reasons chatbots are gaining popularity in lead generation is their ability to engage with potential customers in real-time. Unlike traditional lead generation methods that rely on forms and emails, chatbots can provide instant responses to inquiries and guide users through the sales funnel. This instant communication can help capture leads more effectively and increase conversion rates, ultimately leading to more sales for businesses.

Another key advantage of using chatbots for lead generation is their ability to gather valuable data on customers. By analyzing the conversations and interactions with users, businesses can gain insights into customer preferences, pain points, and buying behavior. This data can then be used to personalize marketing campaigns, improve customer service, and ultimately drive more leads and sales.

Furthermore, chatbots can help streamline the lead generation process by qualifying leads automatically. By asking targeted questions and analyzing user responses, chatbots can determine the level of interest and intent to purchase of each lead. This allows businesses to focus their efforts on leads that are more likely to convert, saving time and resources in the long run.

Overall, the rise of chatbots in lead generation presents a valuable opportunity for website owners, marketers, and online marketing professionals to enhance their strategies and drive better results. By leveraging the power of chatbots, businesses can improve their lead generation efforts, engage with customers more effectively, and ultimately boost their bottom line. As the digital landscape continues to evolve, chatbots will undoubtedly play a crucial role in the future of lead generation and online marketing.

Personalization and Customization in Social Media Lead Generation

In today's digital age, personalization and customization have become essential elements in successful social media lead generation strategies. Website owners, marketing professionals, and online marketers must understand the importance of tailoring their content and messaging to resonate with their target audience on a personal level. By creating personalized experiences for users, businesses can increase engagement, build trust, and ultimately drive more leads through social media platforms.

One of the key benefits of personalization and customization in social media lead generation is the ability to create targeted campaigns that speak directly to the needs and interests of individual users. By leveraging data and analytics, marketers can segment their audience based on demographic information, browsing behavior, and engagement history to deliver highly relevant content that resonates with each user. This tailored approach not only increases the likelihood of capturing leads but also helps to foster a deeper connection with potential customers.

Furthermore, personalization and customization allow businesses to stand out in a crowded digital landscape by offering a unique and tailored experience to users. By creating personalized landing pages, targeted ads, and customized messaging, marketers can differentiate their brand and capture the attention of their target audience. This level of personalization not only enhances the user experience but also helps to build brand loyalty and trust, leading to higher conversion rates and increased lead generation.

Another important aspect of personalization and customization in social media lead generation is the ability to track and measure the effectiveness of campaigns in real-time. By analyzing user interactions, engagement metrics, and conversion rates, marketers can gain valuable insights into what resonates with their audience and make data-driven decisions to optimize their lead generation efforts. This iterative approach allows businesses to continuously refine their strategies and improve their results over time.

In conclusion, personalization and customization are powerful tools that can help website owners, marketing professionals, and online marketers generate leads with social media. By creating tailored experiences, targeted campaigns, and data-driven strategies, businesses can increase engagement, build trust, and drive conversions through personalized interactions with their target audience. Embracing personalization and customization in social media lead generation is essential for staying ahead in today's competitive landscape and unlocking the full potential of social media marketing.

The Role of AI in Enhancing Lead Generation Strategies

In today's digital age, the role of artificial intelligence (AI) in enhancing lead generation strategies cannot be overstated. As website owners, marketers, and online marketing professionals in the niche of generating leads with social media, it is crucial to understand how AI can revolutionize the way we attract and engage potential customers.

One of the key benefits of AI in lead generation is its ability to analyze vast amounts of data in real time. By utilizing machine learning algorithms, AI can identify patterns and trends that human marketers may overlook, allowing for more targeted and personalized marketing campaigns. This data-driven approach can help website owners and marketers better understand their audience and tailor their messaging to resonate with potential leads.

Furthermore, AI can automate repetitive tasks and streamline the lead generation process. From email marketing to social media advertising, AI-powered tools can help marketers reach a larger audience more efficiently. By freeing up time and resources, AI allows marketing professionals to focus on developing creative strategies and building relationships with leads, ultimately driving more conversions and sales.

In addition, AI can enhance the customer experience by providing personalized recommendations and assistance. Chatbots powered by AI can engage with website visitors in real time, answering questions and guiding them through the sales funnel. By offering relevant content and support, AI can help nurture leads and move them closer to making a purchase.

Overall, the role of AI in enhancing lead generation strategies is only set to grow in importance. As website owners, marketers, and online marketing professionals in the niche of generating leads with social media, it is crucial to embrace AI technologies and leverage them to drive business growth. By harnessing the power of AI, we can improve targeting, automation, and customer engagement, ultimately leading to more successful lead generation campaigns.

Chapter 8: Conclusion

Recap of Key Strategies for Successful Lead Generation on Social Media

In the fast-paced world of online marketing, generating leads through social media has become an essential strategy for website owners and marketers. To ensure success in this competitive landscape, it is important to recap key strategies for successful lead generation on social media. By understanding these strategies, marketers can effectively reach their target audience and convert them into valuable leads.

The first key strategy is to identify your target audience. Before implementing any lead generation tactics on social media, it is crucial to have a clear understanding of who your ideal customers are. By knowing their demographics, interests, and online behavior, you can tailor your content and messaging to resonate with them. This targeted approach will help you attract high-quality leads that are more likely to convert.

Another important strategy is to create engaging and valuable content. Social media users are constantly bombarded with information, so it is essential to stand out with content that is informative, entertaining, and relevant to your audience. By providing value through your posts, such as helpful tips, industry insights, or exclusive offers, you can capture the attention of potential leads and build trust with them over time.

Consistency is also key when it comes to successful lead generation on social media. Posting sporadically or infrequently will not yield the desired results. To maintain a strong presence and keep your audience engaged, it is important to create a content calendar and stick to a regular posting schedule. By consistently sharing valuable content and engaging with your audience, you can build brand awareness and attract more leads to your website.

In addition to creating valuable content, it is important to leverage different social media platforms to reach a wider audience. Each platform has its own unique features and audience demographics, so it is important to tailor your content and messaging to fit the platform you are using. By diversifying your social media strategy and exploring different platforms, you can increase your chances of reaching potential leads and driving them to your website.

Lastly, monitoring and analyzing your social media performance is essential for optimizing your lead generation efforts. By tracking key metrics, such as engagement rates, click-through rates, and conversion rates, you can identify what is working well and what needs improvement. This data-driven approach will help you refine your social media strategy over time and maximize the effectiveness of your lead generation efforts. By following these key strategies, website owners and marketers can successfully generate leads through social media and drive business growth in today's digital landscape.

Final Thoughts on Cracking the Code to Lead Generation with Social Media

In conclusion, cracking the code to lead generation with social media is a powerful tool for website owners, marketers, and online marketing professionals looking to generate leads. By utilizing social media platforms effectively, businesses can reach a wider audience, engage with potential customers, and ultimately drive more traffic to their websites. It is important for businesses to understand the different social media platforms available and how to tailor their content to each platform in order to maximize their lead generation efforts.

One of the key takeaways from this subchapter is the importance of creating valuable and engaging content that resonates with your target audience. By providing valuable information, entertaining content, or exclusive offers, businesses can attract and retain followers who are more likely to convert into leads. Additionally, businesses should utilize social media analytics tools to track the performance of their content and make data-driven decisions to optimize their lead generation efforts.

Another key point to consider is the importance of building relationships with your audience on social media. By engaging with followers, responding to comments and messages, and participating in conversations, businesses can foster trust and credibility with their audience. This, in turn, can lead to increased brand loyalty and higher conversion rates.

Furthermore, businesses should not underestimate the power of social media advertising in their lead generation strategies. By targeting specific demographics, interests, and behaviors, businesses can reach potential customers who are more likely to be interested in their products or services. Social media advertising can be a cost-effective way to reach a larger audience and drive more traffic to your website.

In conclusion, cracking the code to lead generation with social media requires a strategic and holistic approach. By creating valuable content, building relationships with your audience, and utilizing social media advertising, businesses can effectively generate leads and drive more traffic to their websites. By implementing the strategies outlined in this subchapter, website owners, marketers, and online marketing professionals can harness the power of social media to grow their businesses and achieve their lead generation goals.

www.ingramcontent.com/pod-product-compliance
Lightning Source LLC
Chambersburg PA
CBHW070957220526
45471CB00007B/3067